# THE FUTURE OF COMMUNICATIONS:

## FROM TEXTING TO AUGMENTED REALITY

BY AILYNN COLLINS

CONTENT CONSULTANT:

PETER C. BISHOP, PH.D., APF

TEACH THE FUTURE.ORG

HOUSTONFUTURES.ORG

**CAPSTONE PRESS**
a capstone imprint

Captivate is published by Capstone Press, an imprint of Capstone.
1710 Roe Crest Drive, North Mankato, Minnesota 56003
www.capstonepub.com

**Library of Congress Cataloging-in-Publication Data is available on the Library of Congress website.**
ISBN 978-1-5435-9219-1 (library binding)
ISBN 978-1-4966-6623-9 (paperback)
ISBN 978-1-5435-9223-8 (eBook PDF)

Summary: Describes what the future may hold in the realm of communications, including technological advancements and human impact.

**Photo Credits**
Newscom: Blend Images/Donald Iain Smith, 33, Deng Hua Xinhua News Agency, 35, Image China, 15, ZUMA Press/Ferrari, 29, (Top); Shutterstock: Ahmet Misirligul, 27, Blue Planet Studio, 21, Dean Drobot, 9, fim.design, 7, (Bottom), fizkes, 7, (Top), Fotos593, 29, (Bottom), Frederic Legrand - COMEO, 41, GaudiLab, 43, George W. Bailey, 37, (Top), Love the wind, 5, Lucy Brown - loca4motion, 39, Mark Nazh, 31, metamorworks, 17, , 19, Milles Studio, Cover, Pressmaster, 25, Rawpixel.com, 13, RHJPhtotoandilustraion, 11, Selenophile, 23, Vantage_DS, 37, (Bottom)

**Design Elements**
Shutterstock: nanmulti, Zeynur Babayev

**Editorial Credits**
Editor: Mandy Robbins; Designer: Kay Fraser; Media Researcher: Jo Miller; Production Specialist: Laura Manthe

All internet sites appearing in back matter were available and accurate when this book was sent to press.

Printed in the United States of America.
PA100

# TABLE OF CONTENTS

Words in bold are in the glossary.

# COMMUNICATION IN A CHANGING WORLD

Today, cell phones are part of everyday life. But if you had been alive 50 years ago, your telephone would've been attached to a wall. You would have dialed each digit of a number one at a time on a spinning wheel. If you had the latest phone, you might have pressed buttons instead of dialing the number.

Everything changed on a spring day in 1973. Martin Cooper shocked people by making a phone call in the middle of a New York City street. He was using the first cell phone. It was the size of a brick. This was the beginning of the cell phones we have today.

If you had one of those first cell phones, you wouldn't have been able to text or video chat. You couldn't share your photos or update your status on social media. Communication has changed a lot since that time.

A modern-day cell phone compared to an old rotary phone

Cell phones connect people everywhere through text, voice, and video. Most phones are small enough to fit in a pocket. People rarely go anywhere without them. They take photos on their phones and share those photos with friends. They can keep in touch with others no matter where they are.

Many new words have been invented as modern communication has changed. People download or upload content, tweet, chat, or post updates on social media. They **stream** and save things on the **cloud**. They use emojis.

With all of these changes, you may wonder how people will communicate in the future. What will connecting with others look like in 10 years? What about in 30 years?

## FACT:

Martin Cooper was inspired by the TV show *Star Trek* to invent the first cell phone. The characters used "communicators" to talk to people anywhere in space.

Today people take for granted that cell phones let them connect with others anywhere and at any time.

Emojis are a fun way to communicate with pictures instead of words.

# CHAPTER 1
# WHAT IS JUST AHEAD?

Cell phones have gone from being only telephones to becoming small portable computers. People can text, email, video chat, and play games on them. They can even stream TV and movies. What's next? How will phones change in the next few years?

Cell phone improvements in the near future will probably make them work better. Phones will be easier to use. Phones will also be harder to break and more **resistant** to water damage. They will have longer-lasting batteries, more memory, and a faster **processing speed**.

Phones will probably have even more features. Many new phones will have three or more cameras and lenses. These features will work together to take better photos. They'll be able to zoom out far or up close. They'll also be better at recognizing the owner's face for greater security. Phones will probably be less expensive too.

People used to carry cameras with them to take pictures.
Now they can just use a cell phone.

## FLEXIBLE PHONES

When it comes to video chatting, searching the internet, or watching movies on a phone, everyone wants a bigger screen. But no one wants a bigger, clumsier phone. To solve this problem, some phone companies are making cell phones that have screens that will bend or fold. The Huawei company in China believes that by 2021, half of their phones will be foldable.

## ENVIRONMENTALLY FRIENDLY

Having an environmentally friendly phone is a good way to take care of the planet. Discarded phones, like all garbage, can clog up landfills. Some chemicals in them can even harm the environment. Companies are now trying to use **nontoxic** materials when they make phones so that they create less pollution. Green phones would use less energy and have more efficient batteries. Some companies have already created **solar**-powered cell phones. Perhaps one day, that will be more common. In the future, phones could also be recyclable.

vid: day 09/2020
0345, edit.

Bendable phones would make big screens easy to carry.

## SECURITY

With people storing so much of their personal information digitally, cell phone security is important. From phones that can read fingerprints to those that recognize faces, security is becoming more personal. In the future, a phone might recognize a person through the map of blood vessels in his or her hand. Everyone's blood vessel pattern is different. A phone could recognize its owner's pattern. Only that person would be able to unlock it.

# BANDWIDTH

Has your phone ever dropped a call? Has your video chat frozen? These things happen because of limited **bandwidth**. Bandwidth is the amount of information that can be sent or received in a certain amount of time. It is measured in bits per second (bps). It determines how quickly a phone is able to send or receive messages or download an app or a movie.

How does more bandwidth help phones work better? Imagine you have to transfer water from one bowl to another through a narrow straw. It will take a while for the water to make it into the second bowl. If you replaced the thin straw with a wider one, the water would flow through more quickly. That is what increasing bandwidth does for data.

Today phones run on 4G networks. 4G stands for "fourth generation." In the past, phones had 3G or 2G networks. With 3G, if someone wanted to download a movie, it could take hours. With 4G it takes about 6 minutes.

Increasing bandwidth would make video chatting much clearer and more reliable.

# A FASTER NETWORK

What's faster than 4G? If you guessed 5G, you're right. Companies all over the world are racing to be the first to roll out this new network.

A 5G network would be 100 times faster than 4G. It would allow for ultra fast downloads. Smart devices could communicate quickly with one another. Self-driving cars could get real-time information as they traveled. Cell phones would work much faster.

But switching to 5G has its challenges. This system would work differently than 4G. With 4G, data is carried inside cables that connect to large cell towers. The towers send signals through the air to phones. A signal can travel about 10 miles (16 km) with 4G. If someone is too far from a cell tower, his or her phone won't work very well.

### FACT:
With a 4G network, the internet responds to commands in 45 milliseconds. With 5G, it would take 1 millisecond. That's 400 times faster than a blink of an eye!

With a 5G network, devices and machines that are connected to the internet could communicate with each other in a split second.

With 5G, there would be no cables. Cell signals would travel through the air. They would be connected by radio devices called small cell antennae. But a 5G signal can travel only about 1,000 feet (304 meters). These antenna boxes would have to be installed on posts every 1,000 feet (304 m) in all neighborhoods. This would be easier in cities than it would be in rural areas.

Setting up a 5G network is also very expensive. Internet carrier companies would have to rebuild a whole new network. It would take time. Everyone would have to buy new phones too. 4G phones cannot run on a 5G network.

Right now, China seems to be at the front of the 5G race. It has already begun to put antenna boxes in major cities. Experts think that by 2025, the United States will have half of all households on 5G, especially those living in cities.

In the next 10 years, most cities in the United States could be connected to a 5G network.

It looks like 5G is the future of communication. If the current trends in technology continue, people will depend more and more on their devices. Robots, computers, and phones could play a bigger role in people's lives. Self-driving cars and buses may become the normal way to get around. Drones could deliver packages and letters. Robots might help customers at stores. This would all be possible with a 5G network. People might even communicate using **virtual reality** (VR). They could send **avatars** into virtual rooms to talk to others.

## A CONNECTED WORLD

Devices that are connected to the internet communicate with one another in order to work more smoothly. This is called the "Internet of Things" (IoT). Phones can connect to home security systems to keep watch when people are out. Fitness trackers, smart fire alarms, and even smart refrigerators are all part of the IoT. With a 5G network, there could be more devices than people connected to the internet, communicating all the time.

Self-driving cars could rely on a 5G network to communicate with one another and make split-second decisions while driving.

# SOCIAL MEDIA

In the past, if someone had news to share or an opinion to give, they might make a phone call, write a letter, or send an email. It would take time, and the news would usually go to a small group of people.

Social media has changed the way news is spread. Today people can share news and information as soon as it happens. They can comment and give their opinions on matters immediately. And they can share it not just with their friends and family, but also with strangers. News spreads faster and can go all over the world.

In the United States, it is estimated that 244 million people use social media every day. Worldwide, about 4 billion people use the internet to communicate. As this number increases, internet companies want to change the way people use social media. They want to make it easier for people to share videos. Soon people will be able to use voice commands to post what they want to say.

Social media has caused a huge shift from face-to-face communication to online communication.

Social media has also become important in forming communities. People with the same interests meet online. Many people consider these connections friends, even if they've never met in person. This trend is likely to continue. Social media will likely continue to be a main way people interact with one another in the future.

Experts believe that social media will also be a better place for advertising. In the past, print magazines and newspapers, television, and radio were the main places that companies advertised their products. But social media and online streaming of music, movies, and television shows have made those mediums less popular. The biggest trend in advertising now involves people called social media influencers. These social media stars have thousands of friends or followers. Companies offer them free products. Influencers post videos or photos of themselves using the products. Their followers may even get a special code for a discount on the product. This trend is likely to grow.

Anyone can become a social media influencer if they get enough online followers.

## ONLINE DANGERS

Communicating online has many benefits, but it also has dangers. People need to learn how to tell if information they see online is true or false. They have to be aware of online bullying, called cyberbullying, and learn how to prevent or fight against it. As technology increases online communication, what other dangers could arise? Humans can suffer from a lack of physical interaction. It's important to think about these challenges so that we can find solutions before problems become more difficult to solve.

# MEETINGS

Another way people communicate is in meetings. Students have school projects to discuss. Adults have meetings to attend for work. Someone may need to meet with a doctor, therapist, or lawyer. In any of these situations, if someone can't meet in person, a video meeting can come in handy. Unfortunately, there are some challenges with video meetings today. Connections sometimes fail. Videos can be grainy and unclear. Sound quality is often poor.

Better technology for streaming video, such as a 5G network, would make these meetings clearer without interruptions. Large groups of people could meet easily from their computers or their phones from any corner of the world. It would feel as if they were talking to people next door. If a doctor needed medical information from a patient, the patient might be able to attach a special device to his or her phone. It could scan the person's body and immediately send that information to the doctor.

Online meetings mean that students don't need to be together to work together on a group project.

# CHAPTER 2

# WHAT DOES THE FUTURE HOLD?

Improvements in technology can happen quickly. In the next 20 to 30 years, communication will probably be familiar, but different. Many new ideas that are being worked on today might be common then.

## WEARABLE TECHNOLOGY

Today most people go everywhere with their phones. But they're so easy to lose. What if you never had to worry about that?

Devices such as smartwatches are becoming more popular. They can send and receive messages just like phones. There are also smart glasses. These glasses are actually small computers and phones. They respond to voice commands and are hands-free communication. Today these devices are still new and not yet popular. In the future, they may be easier to use, less bulky, and more affordable.

To go one step further, people might one day wear contact lenses that are also communication devices. The lenses would deliver messages, keep track of appointments, and show a daily schedule. It would almost be like you were part computer!

In the future, smart devices could make holograms of information appear before your eyes.

In the next 20 to 30 years, it's likely that mobile devices will be attached to jewelry or clothing. Can you imagine a phone disguised as a necklace or sewn into a jacket?

In the future, clothing could have all kinds of technology built into it. You might have a T-shirt with a **global positioning system** (GPS) built in. The shirt might vibrate to tell you which way to go. Clothes could also monitor a person's mood or health. This information could then be passed on to doctors or family members.

Jewelry tech could keep track of your heart rate, blood pressure, and overall health. When it detects a health problem, it could give advice, send for help, or make a doctor's appointment.

Don't forget that no matter where they are kept, devices need power. Wearable tech could have unique ways to power batteries. Shoes might convert your physical activity to a type of energy that could charge your batteries. Batteries might also be charged using body heat or solar energy.

Future tech may include smart watches and necklaces.

Shoppers may one day access their credit cards using smart rings.

# VIRTUAL REALITY

VR is a three-**dimensional** (3D) interactive experience. Users can enter a computer-generated world using special goggles. They act or react to whatever is happening there. With VR, people can interact even when they cannot meet in person.

As VR tech improves, the goggles will likely be replaced by smaller devices. People might even have rooms with special cameras. These cameras could project people into a virtual meeting room. Each person could appear as though he or she were actually in the room. People could also create avatars and send them to the meetings. The avatars would move and speak as if they were the real person. Perhaps in the future, schools will offer virtual attendance. When students are ill or injured, they could participate in class through VR.

## FACT:
VR is not new tech. One of the earliest forms of VR is a flight simulator, created in the 1920s. In 1962, a machine called the Sensorama was used to show a VR-type movie.

Today, VR goggles let you see fairly realistic images in 3D.
In the future, what you see might look completely real.

# A 3D PHONE: HOLOGRAMS

People see and experience the world in 3D. Phones display pictures and videos in 2D. Holograms could give phones the ability to display images in 3D.

Imagine you could send your friends a photo of the dinosaur skeleton you're looking at in a museum. When they receive it, the image would pop out of their phone screens and they would see the dinosaur just as if they were there. This is what holograms could do.

Phone companies thought that holograms would be a common feature of cell phones by the early 2000s. But it turned out to be more difficult than expected. Today companies such as Red Hydrogen have devices with images that appear to be in 3D. The images are still flat, but they can be seen from several angles. True hologram technology is still in the research phase. It may take another 20 years to perfect.

One day people might see holograms of each other while video chatting.

# UNIVERSAL TRANSLATION

Today social media can translate a post from one language to another by clicking a link that says, "See translation." But imagine you could talk with someone who speaks a different language and understand what they're saying immediately. There are a few translation apps in use today that attempt to do this. Future devices will probably be faster and more accurate.

In the future, phones may come with apps that will translate a foreign language speaker's words in real time. This technology could also be able to translate common expressions and slang, or informal language. Today's apps aren't yet able to do this.

There may also be earpieces that you can fit into your ears. When you meet people who speak a different language, your earpiece would translate as they speak. And when you speak back, the other person's device would translate your words into their language. This way, everyone in the world could understand one another.

Translation apps could effectively tear down the language barrier between people of different cultures.

## FACT:

Currently, devices need to be told what languages are being translated. In the future, devices might instantly recognize what language is being spoken.

# ARTIFICIAL INTELLIGENCE IN COMMUNICATION

Have you ever asked a phone or computer a question? Did it give you the right answer within seconds? This is an example of **artificial intelligence** (AI). You might know it as Siri, Cortana, Alexa, or Google. In the future, there will be many more.

AI devices can communicate with one another at much faster speeds than humans can speak. This ability helps them perform many tasks. AI robots clean homes. AI also helps doctors detect and fight diseases. Right now, many vehicles have self-driving features, which are another form of AI. In the future, most cars may be entirely self-driving, and they could communicate with one another to prevent accidents and control the flow of traffic.

As AI technology improves, communication will change. People may simply speak to their devices which could pass messages along to others. Today people often ask questions of their home hubs. They use voice-to-text features on their phones. In the future, entire conversations could happen without people speaking directly to one another.

Amazon's Echo Dot AI device

Google Home AI device

# CONNECT THE WORLD

People who live in **remote** areas often have a difficult time accessing the internet or getting a cell phone signal. They live far from any cell towers and must use satellite internet. A small dish in their house gets a signal from a satellite in space. The satellite gets its signal from the internet provider. But current satellite internet can't reach everyone. That could change in the future. Currently there are thousands of satellites in space. They do jobs that include GPS guidance, communications, and taking photos for national security. Yet there are not enough so that everyone in the world has access to the internet.

In 2019, a company called SpaceX launched 60 small communications satellites into orbit around the earth. This launch was the first of many to come. Eventually, companies like SpaceX plan to have thousands of these satellites in orbit. They will connect to each other and to places all over the earth, bringing internet access and communication to everyone.

Other companies such as Amazon, OneWeb, and Telesat are planning on doing the same. Even though these satellites are launching now or in the near future, they will not be in full use for many years. There are still challenges, such as building receivers to get signals from the satellites.

People in remote areas such as rural Mongolia rely on satellites for cell signals and internet access.

# [HAPTER 3

# WHAT IS WAY OUT THERE?

Futures studies experts are called foresight professionals or futurists. They use social science and imagination to create different **scenarios**, or examples, of what the future could hold. They have some interesting ideas for what communication might look like in 30 years or more.

Dr. Michio Kaku, a professor at the City University of New York, believes that the future could bring about a type of internet called the "brain-net." Instead of sharing ideas and news, people could share emotions and memories. Other futurists believe that people may be able to share their dreams with others too.

Facebook founder Mark Zuckerberg believes that the future of communication will not be spoken or written. He says people will be able to think a command to their devices, and the devices will obey. Early experiments suggest that this might be possible.

Commanding devices with your thoughts will take at least 30 years to perfect. This could mean that a computer chip would be implanted into a person's head in order to send thoughts to their devices.

Other futurists believe that people will spend increasingly more time in virtual reality worlds. VR tech could advance so much that people could feel as though they are touching each other in the virtual world.

Mark Zuckerberg

# AN UNKNOWN FUTURE

From cell phones to social media, present-day communication would've sounded like fantasies to people who lived 100 years ago. Who knows how much will change by the year 2120?

Some futurists believe that humans will become more dependent on AI. They might add so much tech to their bodies that they'd almost become part human, part machine. They could be connected to the internet all the time, whether they have a device or not. They could watch any show or movie any time they want through a contact lens. They could shake hands over a business deal in another country without ever leaving home.

Other futurists think that all the tech that exists in the future will be similar to what we have today. It will be better, but it won't change how people live.

There are even experts who believe that humans may decide to turn their backs on technology altogether and return to using pen and paper. Which prediction do you think is most likely?

Future tech might include touch screens built into
the walls of buildings.

# TIMELINE

**1973** > Martin Cooper exhibits the first cellular phone.

**1979** > 1G network begins in Tokyo, Japan.

**1983** > Motorola launches the world's first cell phone, the DynaTAC 800x.

**1989** > Motorola introduces the first flip phones.

**1991** > The internet becomes available to the public.

**1992** > Cell phones offer the first texting feature.

**1993** > The IBM Simon becomes the first touch screen smartphone.

**2007** > Apple sells the first iPhone.

**2012** > Google invents the first smart glasses.

**2019** > SpaceX launches the first of its communication satellites.

# FUTURE POSSIBILITIES

**2021** > Half of the cell phones made in China may be foldable.

**2025** > Half of U.S. homes could have 5G.

**2025** > Virtual reality may be used in most households.

**2025** > Universal translation could make it so that everyone on Earth can understand one another.

**2030** > Cell phones could be implanted into the body.

**2030** > Holograms in cell phones may become widespread.

**2050** > People may communicate with their devices through their minds.